Manthan

Introspection Within

Meenakshi

BookLeaf Publishing

India | USA | UK

Made with ❤ on the BookLeaf Publishing Platform
www.bookleafpub.in
www.bookleafpub.com

Dedication

To my parents,

who always believed in me,

even when the path seemed unclear.

Your unwavering faith, endless support,

and unconditional love

have been the foundation

of every dream I've pursued.

This book is a testament to the strength,

hope, and resilience you've instilled in me.

Thank you for being my guiding light,

my inspiration, and my greatest champion.

I owe it all to you.

Acknowledgment

Writing poetry is a deeply personal and often solitary journey, yet bringing a collection to life is an act of collaboration. I am profoundly grateful to all those who have supported me in this process of creating this book.

First and foremost, I want to express my heartfelt gratitude to my family and friends, whose unwavering love and encouragement have been my constant source of strength, guiding me through every moment of doubt. Your belief in me has given me the courage to continue exploring the depths of my thoughts and emotions through poetry.

I am equally grateful to my mentors and teachers, whose wisdom and guidance have helped me hone my craft. Your insights have pushed me to dig deeper and to strive for greater authenticity in my writing. You have shown me the value of digging deeper, not just into words, but into the very essence of what I seek to express.

Finally, I acknowledge the quiet, persistent voice within me that calls me to write. It is by listening to this voice that I have found clarity, and it is through this voice that these poems have come into being.

To everyone who has been a part of this journey, thank you. *Manthan - An Introspection Within* is as much yours as it is mine.

Preface

Manthan - An Introspection Within is a journey into the depths of the human mind and soul.

Poetry is the language of the soul, a mirror reflecting the innermost thoughts and emotions that often go unspoken. In a world that rushes forward at an unforgiving pace, introspection becomes a rare and precious act. *Manthan - An Introspection Within* is an invitation to pause, reflect, and journey inward.

This collection was born in moments of solitude, where thoughts flowed freely and emotions surfaced without restraint. It is a tapestry woven with threads of joy and sorrow, hope and despair, love and longing-each poem a fragment of a deeper truth.

But this book is more than a collection of poems. It is a call to self-discovery, a companion for those seeking meaning in the quiet spaces of their own minds. Whether you find solace, inspiration, or a new perspective within these pages, may this book guide you on your journey of introspection. And as you read these poems, may you find moments of connection and resonance, inspiring you to engage in your introspective journey—one that leads you closer to understanding the truths that reside within.

 Meenakshi (Minzi)
August 2024

Life is Tough but I Am Tougher

In the shadows where the wild winds wail,
Life throws its storms, a relentless gale.
Mountains rise, and valleys sink deep,
Yet within my heart, a fire does seep.

Through winding roads where doubt likes to
creep,
I lace up my boots, ready not just to leap.
For every bruise life etches on my soul,
I gather my strength, I reclaim control.

The thorns may prick, the darkness may bite,
But I stand my ground, fueled by inner light.
With every setback, I learn to stand tall,
Challenges form the mold of us all.

The world may be heavy, a burden to bear,
But I carry my dreams, a testament rare.
In moments of silence, when fear grips tight,
I whisper to myself, "Keep going—you've
fought the good fight."

Each trial a lesson, each tear a brick laid,
Building a fortress where fear can't invade.
The road might be rugged, with stones that
may sting,
But I forge my path, in the joy that I bring.

So let the winds howl, let the shadows
intrude,
I'll weather the tempest, with courage
imbued.
Life is a canvas, wild, untamed, and rare,
Yet I paint it boldly, with colors so rare.

For every challenge that seeks to deter,
I rise with resolve—life is tough, but I'm tougher.
With each passing day, I'll embrace what's in store,
For the heart of a warrior knows how to soar.

Who Will Cry When You Die

When the final breath escapes your lips,
And life's last chapter gently slips,
Who will cry, who will grieve,
In the wake of what you leave?

Will tears fall from eyes once bright,
In memory of your guiding light?
Will hearts feel the aching loss,
Of a soul who bore life's cross?

Will they speak of the love you gave,
Of how you taught them to stand, be brave?
Will they remember the kindest deeds,
The way you met their deepest needs?

Or will the world keep spinning on,
As if you had never truly gone?
Will your absence be a silent mark,
In a world that never felt your spark?

It's not the wealth or fame you gain,
But the lives you touch, the love you sustain,
The way you lift, the way you care,
The moments of joy, the burdens you bear.

So live a life that's rich and true,
In every action, in all you do,
For when you're gone, it's not the sighs,
But the hearts you've warmed that will cry.

In the echoes of the love you spread,
The lives you brightened, the words you said,
Those who've known you, near and far,
Will cry for the loss of a shining star.

For, in the end, it's not goodbye,
But the love you leave that will never die,
And those who cry will remember well,
The story of a life lived with love to tell.

I Have Learnt to Live Alone

I have learned to live alone,
In quiet spaces, I've made my home,
Where echoes of my thoughts still reside,
And solitude walks by my side.

The world outside may rush and roar,
But here within, I crave no more,
In the silence, I find my peace,
A gentle calm, a sweet release.

I've learned to cherish my own company,
In moments of stillness, I roam free,
To dream, to think, to simply be,
A soul at rest, in harmony.

No longer do I fear the night,
For in the dark, I find my light,
A glow within that softly shines,
In this space, the world feels mine.

I've found a strength I never knew,
In the quiet, in the view,
Of life unfolding, day by day,
In my way, I'll find my way.

I've learned that being alone is not a curse,
But a gift to know myself first,
To listen to the whispers of my heart,
To embrace each day as a work of art.

I stand alone, but not in vain,
For in this solitude, I gain,
A deeper love, a clearer sight,
A life that's lived in my light.

So here I am, alone yet whole,
At peace with self, at peace with soul,
I've learned to live, to stand, to grow,
In the quiet, I've found my flow.
The conflict between heart and mind

In the quiet chambers of my soul,
A battle rages, fierce and whole,
Where heart and mind in conflict lie,
Each pulled at the other's tie.

The heart, a beacon, warm and free,
It beats with passions bold and fierce,
It yearns for dreams, for love's embrace,
And dances in its sacred space.

Yet the mind, a quiet sage,
Seeks reason's light on every page,
It weighs the choices, plans the course,
And steers my path with measured force.

The heart will whisper, "Follow dreams,"
To chase the stars, to hear love's gleams,
While the mind will argue, "Pause and see,
Is this the right path for thee?"

The heart will sing of joy and grace,
Of moments fleeting, of time to chase,
But the mind will counter, calm and wise,
"Consider all, be cautious, analyze."

A storm of feelings and thoughts collide,
In this internal, restless tide,
Where passions fight with logic's hand,
And each must seek a place to stand.

The heart desires to soar and fly,
To reach for the stars in the sky.
The mind insists on ground and pace,
To chart the course, to find a space.

Yet in this struggle, there's a chance,
For both to join in life's great dance,
To blend the dreams with reasoned might,
To find a path that feels just right.

So here I stand, with heart and mind,
In harmony, I seek to bind,
To navigate the storms that roll,
With both my heart and mind as soul.

Together they will light my way,
Through every night, through every day.
In the conflict, I'll find my blend,
Where heart and mind in peace transcend.

In the quiet chambers where shadows blend,
A battle rages, where thoughts ascend.
The heart, a tempest of wild, sweet cries,
The mind, a compass with rational ties.

The heart, it dances in dreams untold,
Whispers of love, both tender and bold.
It beckons forth with a vibrant thrill,
A siren's call, an enchanting will.

"Oh, dare to leap, to trust and to feel,
Embrace the chaos; let passion heal.
For life is fleeting, a moment's guise,
In the warmth of love, eternity lies."

But the mind, astute, with steady gaze,
Counters with logic, a cautious maze.
"Step back, dear heart, consider the road,
Life's not a melody, nor an eased load.

Think of the burdens, the scars that remain,
The echoes of sorrow, the lessons of pain.
What of the future? The paths left to tread?
With reason as a guide, tread lightly instead."

And so they clash, in this inner refrain,
The heart's fervent song versus reason's chain.
Each coin has two sides, a dance of the soul,
A pull and a push, a constant patrol.

Yet in this discord, a truth finds its place,
Both heart and mind wear a delicate grace.
For love needs the wisdom that reason can
bring,
While courage ignites what the heart dares to
sing.

So let them converse, let their voices entwine,
In the tapestry woven of both heart and
mind.
Conflict, when embraced, can lead to the
spark
That lights the way home from the depths of
the dark.

It's Me in the Mirror

It's me in the mirror, a face I know,
With eyes that reflect the years that grow,
A story written in lines and light,
A journey captured in day and night.

I see the dreams that still reside,
The hopes and fears I've learned to hide,
A silent strength, a quiet grace,
In every curve, in every trace.

The mirror shows what others miss,
The battles fought, the moments of bliss,
The laughter that lines my eyes with gold,
The tears that have stories left untold.

It's me in the mirror, standing tall,
In every flaw, I see it all,
The scars that tell of lessons learned,
The fires through which I've fiercely burned.

I see the child I used to be,
The one who dreamt so endlessly,
And now the woman, strong and true,
Who's faced the storms and made it through?

In the mirror, I meet my gaze,
A thousand thoughts in a single phase,
But most of all, I see my soul,
Complete, imperfect, yet beautifully whole.

It's me in the mirror, nothing to hide,
With all my truths laid laid open wide,
A reflection of all I've come to be,
A portrait of my own decree.

So I stand and smile at the sight I see,
For in that glass, it's truly me,
A soul still growing, still becoming,
A story still unfolding, humming.

Its ok not to be ok

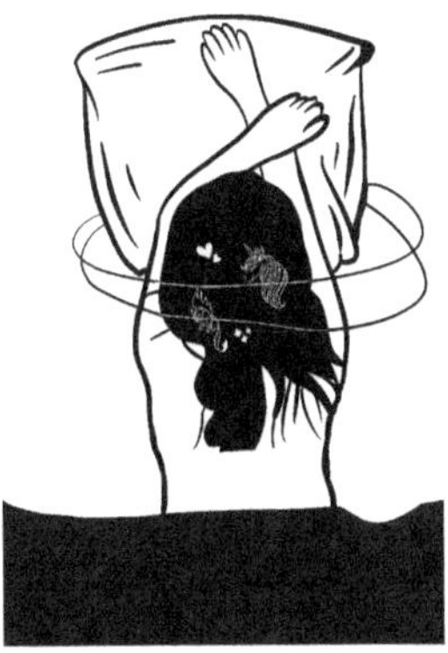

It's okay not to be okay,
To feel the weight, the strain, the fray,
To stumble on life's winding road,
And carry a heavy, unseen load.

It's okay when tears begin to fall,
When you feel like you've lost it all,
To sit with sadness, let it stay,
For even pain must have its day.

It's okay to pause, to take a breath,
To feel the ache, the fear of death,
To wonder if you'll find your way,
In the darkness that shades your day.

It's okay not to have all the answers,
To dance with doubt, with life's dancers,
To question why, to search for meaning,
In a world that's often unredeeming.

It's okay to lean, to ask for aid,
To share the burden, feel afraid,
For strength is not just standing tall,
But knowing when to crawl.

It's okay to be lost for a while,
To lose your spark, to fake your smile,
For even in the deepest night,
The stars will guide you back to light.

It's okay not to be okay,
To embrace the mess, the disarray,
For in the chaos, you will find,
The courage to be gentle and kind.

So give yourself the grace to feel,
To let the wounds take time to heal,
It's okay not to be okay,
For even the strongest hearts give way.

The love that faded over the years

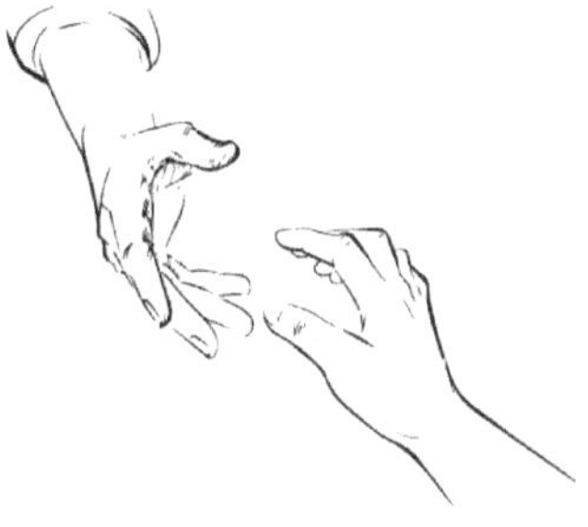

Once, our love was bright and bold,
A story in colors, a tale untold,
But time, it wove its quiet thread,
And slowly, the vibrant hues went dead.

We danced in the fire, hearts ablaze,
In every touch, in passion's gaze,
But as the seasons changed their tune,
Our love began to wane, to swoon.

The whispers that once filled the night,
Grew faint and cold, lost their light,
The laughter that echoed through the halls,
Faded away, as silence calls.

Promises made in the heat of youth,
Were tested by time, by life's cruel truth,
And somewhere along the winding way,
The love we knew began to stray.

We held on tight, we tried to fight,
But something shifted, out of sight,
The spark that once ignited our dreams,
Dwindled to ash in quiet streams.

Now, we sit in the stillness, aware,
Of the love that was, but is no longer there,
The memories linger, sweet and clear,
But the passion's gone, replaced by fear.

We've grown apart, yet still we stand,
Two souls adrift, no longer hand in hand,
The love we had, now just a shade,
A faded echo, a promise frayed.

But even as the love decays,
There's beauty in the time, the days,
We shared a moment, a chapter dear,
In a book that's closed, yet still held near.

So here's to the love that once was bright,
That faded slowly, into the night,
Though it's gone, it left its mark,
A quiet glow, a softened spark.

Your shadows will also leave you one day

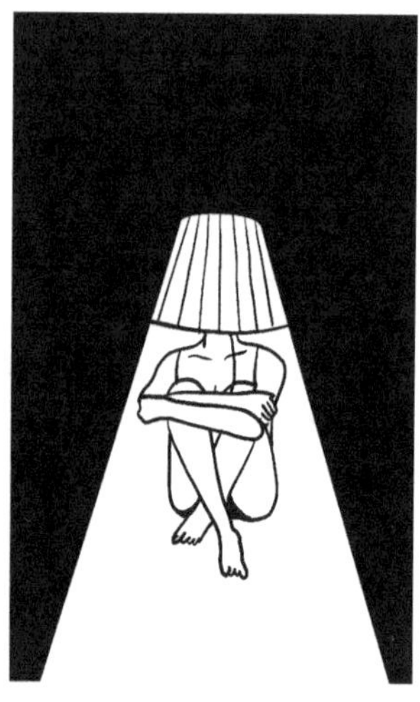

In the twilight's gentle glow,
Where whispers of the day bestow,
A story of shadows quietly unfolds,
In the dance of dusk, a truth untold.

Beneath the sun's embracing reign,
We move through joy, we wade through pain,
Our shadows trail, an echo near,
A silent witness, calm and clear.

But as the stars lay claim to the sky,
And the moon takes its watch on high,
Realize, my friend, that time shall sever,
The ties of this bond, now and forever.

For shadows are fickle, they twist and bend,
A fleeting companion that time may suspend.
Through dusk and dawn, they seem so true,
Yet they fade, like dreams, into the blue.

In moments of laughter, in tears, we've bled,
The shadow reflects what the heart once said.
Yet as seasons change, and the years grow old,
A poignant farewell, as memories unfold.

Embrace the light, let it guide your soul,
For shadows are whispers, never the whole.
Cherish the days when they dance by your
side,
But know they will wane, like the ocean's tide.

So walk with your shadow, while it feels near,
Bask in the warmth of the sun, let go of your
fear.
Just know as you travel this life's winding
way,
Your shadow will also leave you one day.

And when it departs, don't mourn what's
gone,
For the essence of light will forever live on.
In the heart of the night, in the dawn's soft
embrace,
The shadows may shift, yet love leaves its
trace.

The things you see only when you slow down

In the rush of life, the world flies by,
A blur of colors, a whispered sigh.
But pause for a moment, take a breath,
And see what hides in the stillness beneath.

The sun sets slowly in a painted sky,
Its hues unnoticed by the hurried eye.
But when you linger, you start to see,
The dance of light in each trembling tree.

The flutter of wings in a silent grove,
The soft-spoken secrets the wind beholds.
The laughter of children, distant and sweet,
Echoes of joy in the rhythm of your heartbeat.

A flower's bloom in its gentle grace,
The lines of time on an elder's face.
The stories told in the eyes of the wise,
The quiet strength in the tears they disguise.

In the quiet, the world becomes clear,
The beauty in details draws you near.
For life's true wonders aren't meant to be
found,
They're the things you see only when you slow
down.

Don't believe everything you think

In the quiet of the mind, shadows play,
Whispers of doubt dance in disarray.
Thoughts like clouds drift and shift,
Some heavy with rain, others mere mist.

A voice that insists, "You're not enough,"
Echoes in corners, relentless and tough.
It cloaks the truth in a shroud of despair,
But listen closely, there's more to declare.

Like a painter who's certain of hues,
Yet dreads the bold strokes, afraid to choose,
Thoughts may constrict like a vise on your heart,
Yet life's vibrant dance is a complicated art.

Remember the stories that spin in your head,
Some tales bring comfort, while others mislead.
Don't lock up your spirit in thoughts that confine;
Embrace the uncertainty, and let your light shine.

The critic inside, with its shaming decree,
Is a mirror that warps what is, not what can be.
So question the whispers that lurk in the dark,
For truth is a fire, not merely a spark.

In the realm of the mind, perceptions can skew,
What's imagined as fact may not hold.
So breathe in the moment, let clarity grow,
Trust in your essence, let your light show.

So when shadows of doubt threaten to bloom,
Remember, dear heart, there's light beyond
gloom.
Don't believe everything your thoughts may
insist;
You're more than the echoes, you're a
dreamer, a mist.

Conversation with God -

I

I sat beneath the endless sky,
With questions heavy, heart askew.
In silence, I whispered to the night,
"God, are You there? Can You hear me too?"

The wind it stirred, a gentle sigh,
As if the earth itself replied.
And in that moment, soft and clear,
A voice within began to rise.

"I'm here in the rustling of the leaves,
In the breath you take and the air you breathe.
I'm in the sunlight's warm embrace,
In every tear that traces your face.

I walk with you through joy and pain,
Through every loss and every gain.
When shadows fall and fears arise,
I'm the calm within your stormy skies.

Ask your questions, child, don't be afraid,
For I'm the answer in every prayer you've made.
But know the truth, it lies within,
In the quiet corners where you begin.

I'm the love in every kind deed,
The light that guides you when you most need it.
I'm in the laugh that escapes your lips,
And in the silence of the deepest eclipse.

Do not search for Me in far-off lands,
For I'm the one who holds your hands.
In every beat, your heart does sing,
A sacred hymn to everything.

So speak your truth, and hear My own,
For in your soul, you are never alone.
In this sacred, eternal bond,
I'm with you now and far beyond."

I sat there still, beneath the sky,
And felt a peace I'd never known.
For in that whispered, quiet night,
I found that I was not alone.

Conversation with God
-II

In the stillness of twilight, where shadows
softly blend,
I seek the whispers of the divine, my
ever-patient friend.
With questions like the stars, scattered across
the night,
I call out into the silence, yearning for the
light.

"O God, can you hear me?" I ask with a
hopeful heart,
"In a world that spins so swiftly, where do I
even start?
With troubles like the waves, crashing upon
the shore,
How can I find my footing, when I'm unsure
anymore?"

A gentle breeze surrounds me, a voice in the
air,
"Beloved, every journey starts with a single
prayer.
In your heart lies the answer, the strength you
seek to find,
For even in the chaos, you were crafted so
divine.

Embrace the ebb and flow, the joy and pain
combined,
Each moment holds a lesson, a thread of love
entwined.
When darkness clouds your vision, remember
stars still shine,
Trust in the unfolding, for your path is truly
mine."

I close my eyes in wonder, feeling peace
abound,
For every doubt I carry, in love is tightly
wound.
"O God, grant me the courage, to walk this
road unknown,
To trust that in the silence, I am never all
alone."

With every breath I'm weaving, a tapestry of
grace,
In this sacred conversation, I find my rightful
place.
For in the depths of longing, in the questions
that I pose,
I discover in connection, a love that ever
grows.

And so I stand in twilight, where heaven
meets the earth,
In conversation with the Divine, I find my
truest worth.
No longer just a seeker, but a vessel filled with
light,
In every sacred heartbeat, I illuminate the
night.

The city I live in

Beneath the sky's eternal hue,
Where morning breaks in shades anew,
The city stirs, its heartbeats blend,
A symphony that knows no end.

Streets alive with stories told,
Of dreams pursued and futures bold,
Each corner whispers tales of old,
In this city, where life unfolds.

The hustle hums, a constant beat,
As footsteps dance on busy streets,
Yet in the chaos, calm resides,
In quiet parks where peace abides.

The city lights, a starry glow,
Illuminate the paths we know,
From dawn till dusk, from work to play,
This city guides us on our way.

Cultures blend and voices meet,
In markets vibrant, alleys neat,
A tapestry of life unfurls,
In this city, a world of worlds.

Here, I've found my place, my stride,
In bustling streets, I'm not denied,
A sense of home, a space that's mine,
In this city, where dreams align.

Through every season, every change,
The city grows, in constant range,
Of hopes and plans, of joys and fears,
A living story through the years.

So here's to you, my city fair,
In your embrace, I'm always there,
A part of you, as you're of me,
Together, bound in destiny.

Mowgli – My Hearts Delight

In the quiet corners of my life,
Where echoes lingered, voids were rife,
There came a soul with gentle grace,
A little paw, a loving face.

Mowgli, you entered my space,
Filling the void, leaving no trace,
Of the longing that once held me tight,
You brought the dawn, you brought the light.

Your wagging tail, your playful cheer,
Chased away each silent tear,
In your eyes, I found a place,
Where love abounds, where sorrows erase.

You are the child I never knew,
A bond so strong, so pure, so true,
In every bark, in every leap,
You filled my days, you filled my sleep.

No longer did I yearn or weep,
For in your joy, my heart did leap,
You brought the laughter, the warmth, the care,
Mowgli, my dear, you're always there.

In every cuddle, in every sigh,
You filled the gap, you dried my eye,
You are the one who made me whole,
My precious pet, my kindred soul.

Mowgli, you are more than a friend,
You are the love that has no end,
In your presence, my heart found rest,
You filled the void, you are my best.

So here's to you, my furry child,
With eyes so bright, with spirit wild,
In you, I found what I had missed,
A life complete, a heart that's kissed.

Mowgli, my love, my joy, my light,
You filled the vacuum, made things right,
Forever grateful, I'll always be,
For the gift of you, my Mowgli.

Roots of Love

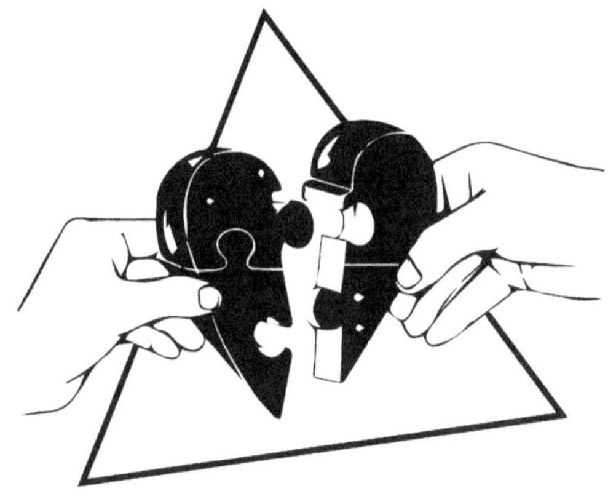

In the garden where my heart was sewn,
With two gentle hands, the seeds were sown.
Whispers of wisdom, soft and clear,
Echo through time, always near.

They brushed my brow with morning light,
Shielded my dreams through the darkest
night.
With every laugh, with every tear,
They shaped my path, they calmed my fear.

Through the maze of life, both straight and
winding,
Their love is a compass, forever binding.
In lessons tough and joys they shared,
An armor forged, a heart prepared.

They showed me kindness, the strength of
grace,
The beauty in each trial we face.
From tiny steps to soaring flights,
Their faith in me is a guiding light.

Though seasons change and years may fly,
The roots run deep, no goodbyes.
In every heartbeat, every song,
I carry their love, where I belong.

So here's to the parents, the brave and true,
In the tapestry of life, I weave them anew.
For all they've given, all they've shown,
In every step, I'm never alone.

I want you to be fearless

I want you to be fearless, my girl,
Like the wind that dances and swirls.
With courage in your heart, so strong,
To stand your ground, where you belong.

I want you to face the world with pride,
With nothing to fear and nothing to hide.
To speak your truth in every space,
With confidence, with grace.

I want you to be bold and brave,
To ride the waves, no longer a slave,
To doubts and fears that may arise—
To see the world through fearless eyes.

I want you to chase your dreams so high,
To spread your wings and touch the sky.
Let no one tell you who you can be,
For you hold the key to your destiny.

I want you to stand tall, unafraid,
In every choice that you have made.
To walk your path with your head held high,
With no regrets, no need to cry.

I want you to know your worth, my dear,
To live your life without any fear.
For you are stronger than you believe,
With so much more that you can achieve.

I want you to embrace each day,
With a fearless heart that leads the way.
For in your courage, you will find,
A world of wonders, beautifully aligned.

I want you to be fearless, my girl,
To let your spirit unfurl.
In every moment, in every dream,
To be the light, the endless beam.

So go, my girl, and take your stand,
With a fearless heart and open hand.
The world is yours to explore,
And I'll be cheering forevermore.

What we eat we become

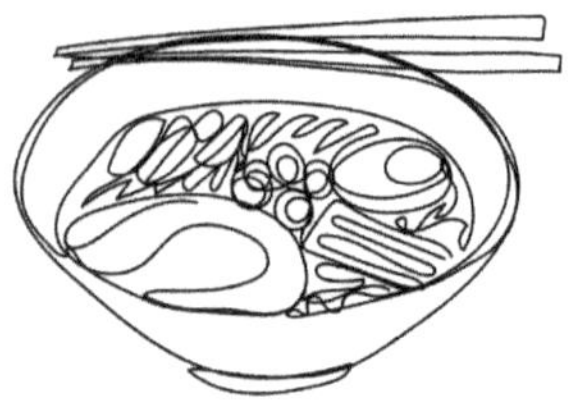

The food we choose, the path we take,
In every bite, a story we make.
The flavors we savor, the textures we delight,
Influencing our bodies, our minds, and our
sight.

The fruit of the earth, a gift so divine,
Nourishing our bodies, making us shine.
The greens that grow, in harmony with
nature's might,
Purifying our bodies, banishing the night.

The grains that grow, in cycles of time,
Providing sustenance, a rhythm sublime.
The legumes that thrive, in rich soil embrace,
Building our strength, in every single place.

The animal's flesh, a gift from above,
A sacrifice made, for our sustenance of love.
But is it just, to take their lives away?
Or can we find compassion, more
deliberately?

The sugary treats are a tempting delight,
But at what cost, to our health and our sight?
Processed foods, a modern convenience true,
But are they worth it, or just a fleeting clue?

MY HERO

In the quiet dawn, when the world's still
asleep,
A silhouette stands and promises to keep.
With calloused hands and a heart of gold,
His stories of courage are timelessly told.

Through trials and storms, like the strongest
oak,
He taught me strength with each word that
he spoke.
His laughter, a melody that brightens the day,
In his warm embrace, all shadows decay.

With wisdom like rivers that endlessly flow,
He's the beacon of hope when the nights feel
so slow.
In the tapestry of life, he weaves threads of
grace,
Each moment shared a cherished embrace.

He's a hero not cloaked in glory or fame,
But in selfless acts, he plays love's sacred
game.
From bicycle rides to the first steps I take,
He's my steadfast guardian, my heart's anchor
stake.

When the path gets rocky, and doubts start to
creep,
He whispers, "Be brave, for the dreams you
must keep."
With every adventure, he lights up the way,
In the book of my life, he's the brightest
display.

So here's to my father, my pillar, my friend,
With gratitude flowing, I cannot pretend.
For in every heartbeat, in each breath, I draw,
He's my hero forever, the best gift of all.

An Ode to My Mom – A Warrior Heart

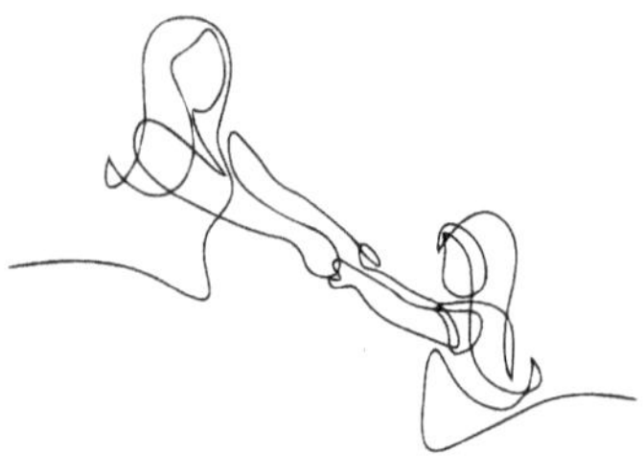

In the quiet dawn, she rises anew,
With a spirit unbroken, fierce, and true.
Though shadows loom and doubts may creep,
In the depths of her heart, her courage runs
deep.

Cancer, a thief, with its dark, cold grip,
Yet she sails through storms on an
unwavering ship.
With laughter as armor, and hope as her
shield,
Against daunting shadows, she refuses to
yield.

Her hands have held fear, and her eyes have
cried tears,
But she's woven a strength far beyond her
years.
Each battle she fought, each moment she
spent,
Was a testament to love, her greatest intent.

In the depths of despair, she found glimmers
of light,
A reason to fight and a will to take flight.
Her dreams are still alive, like stars in the
night,
Guiding her forward, igniting her might.

For every setback, she stands up again,
A phoenix from ashes, she shatters the pain.
With grace in her steps and fire in her soul,
She teaches me how to be brave and be whole.

So here's to my mom, a beacon so bright,
A warrior of heart, a champion of light.
In her battle with shadows, her legacy shows,
That love conquers all, and through darkness,
it grows.

With her laughter like sunshine, her spirit like
spring,
She dances with life, and to hope, she will
cling.
For a mother, a fighter, a dreamer, a friend,
In her story of strength, the light will not end.

Meera My Child – Thank you for choosing US

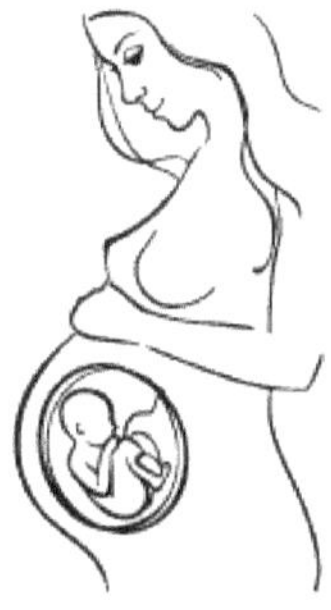

Meera, my child, with a heart so pure,
Thank you for choosing us, of that we're sure.
In the grand design of life's endless play,
You came to us in your own special way.

From the moment you arrived, a light so bright,
You brought a joy that filled our lives with delight.
In your eyes, we saw the stars' gentle gleam,
A promise of love, a beautiful dream.

Thank you, Meera, for the gift you gave,
For the warmth and wonder that we now
crave.
In your laughter, in your tender smile,
We find a love that's endless, all the while.

Through your tiny hands and your first sweet
cries,
We saw a future, a world in your eyes.
In every milestone, every little cheer,
You made our hearts swell with joy and happy
tears.

Thank you for choosing us as your guide,
In this journey of life, where we walk by your
side.
In every lesson learned, in every play,
You've made us proud in every possible way.

Your presence has been a cherished gift,
A reason for our hearts to uplift.
In the moments we share and the love we see,
You've brought us closer to what family can
be.

So here's our thanks, wrapped in endless love,
For the blessing, you are, sent from above.
Meera, our child, with a heart so true,
Thank you for choosing us, for being you.

No Regrets

No regrets, no tears to cry,
No "what ifs" to haunt my mind.
I've lived my life, I've lived it bold,
With every step, I've made my mark.

I've taken risks, I've faced my fears,
And though I've stumbled, I've wiped away
my tears.
I've risen, I've stood tall and strong,
And never once have I felt wrong.

No regrets, no looking back
No second-guessing, no lack of facts.
I've done my best, I've given it all,
And in the end, I stand tall.

I've loved and lost, I've lived and grown,
And through it all, I've learned to let go,
Of the things that held me back,
And the things that made me lack.

No regrets, no regrets to share,
No apologies, no shame to bear.
I've lived my life, I've lived it true,
And with no regrets, I'm free to pursue.

So here's to living life on my terms,
With no regrets, no fear of what's to come.
I'll take the road less traveled, I'll make my
way,
And with every step, I'll face each new day.

Raindrops

Raindrops are falling on my face,
A tender touch, a cool embrace,
Each drop a whisper from the sky,
A secret is shared as they pass by.

They dance upon my skin with grace,
A gentle rhythm I can't chase,
The world slows down, the noise grows still,
As raindrops bend to nature's will.

They kiss my cheeks, they brush my hair,
A fleeting moment, soft and rare,
And in their fall, I find peace,
A quiet joy that brings release.

The clouds may brood, the skies may cry,
But on my face, the tears are dry,
For in the rain, I see the light,
A beauty hidden from plain sight.

Raindrops are falling, and I know,
In every drop, there's life, there's glow,
A fleeting touch of nature's grace,
As raindrops fall upon my face.

You are worth defending

You are worth defending, don't you know?
In every step, in every glow.
You carry strength within your soul,
A quiet fire that makes you whole.

Your heart, your dreams, your voice, your name,
All worth protecting, free from shame.
No fear or doubt can dim your light,
For you are fierce and full of might.

You stand tall, with courage near,
In every breath, you conquer fear.
Your worth is not in what they see,
But in your power, wild and free.

You are worth defending, every part,
Your mind, your body, and your heart.
The world may try to make you small,
But you were made to stand up tall.

So guard your spirit, guard your flame,
Defend your joy, your sacred claim.
For you, dear woman, are strong and true—
No one can take the worth in you.

Believe it now, and know it well,
In every rise, in every fall.
You are worth defending, never forget,
Your power, your grace, is firmly set.

Own Yourself

In every step, in every stride,
There's a power you hold inside.
A force untold, yet strong and bright,
Guiding you through the darkest night.
You are not just what you give,
But in the life you choose to live.
In every dream that's truly yours,
On the strength that reassures.
For in your hands, your heart, your mind,
Lies a worth no one can bind.
Not in their words, not in their gaze,
But in the fire that lights your ways.
So stand tall, with shoulders wide,
For you are more than the world's tide.

Own yourself, own your grace,
And let no fear take your place.
With every challenge, every fall,
You rise again, you stand tall.
Your worth is written in your soul,
A story of strength, a whole heart.

Talk to me Now

Talk to me now, before the time slips by,
Before the stars fade from the evening sky.
Whisper your thoughts, don't let them hide,
In the fleeting moments, stay by my side.

The hours move swiftly, like winds in the
night,
Carrying with them the chance for light.
Hold onto this silence, let's make it loud,
Before time takes us into its shroud.

Talk to me softly, or with urgent cries,
Before the moments vanish, before goodbyes.
Tell me your dreams, your fears untold,
Before they slip away, forever cold.

For time is a thief, with wings of haste,
And words unspoken become dreams
misplaced.
Talk to me now, while we still have today,
Before the time, too soon, flies away.

My silence is not my weakness

In the quiet corners of my mind,
Where shadows dance, and thoughts unwind,
I gather strength in silence deep,
A reservoir of dreams I keep.

My words may fold like fragile wings,
Yet in the hush, a warrior sings.
With every pause, a power grows,
A steady beat, the silence knows.

The world may rush, a roaring tide,
But here within, I choose to bide.
In stillness, there's a potent grace,
A calm resolve, a sacred space.

I listen closely, hear the heart,
The whispers of a vibrant art.
In muted tones, my spirit glows,
For silence nurtures what time sows.

It isn't fear that holds my tongue,
But wisdom's thread that's softly spun.
For eloquence can wear a mask,
But the truth revealed needs no task.

So let them speak, let them proclaim,
In their loud battles, shout my name.
For I will stand, steadfast and wise,
My silence fierce as starlit skies.

With every breath, I choose my peace,
And in that stillness, fears release.
I rise not from the noise around,
But from the silence I have found.

So know this truth, and know it well,
In quietude, my spirit dwells.
My silence is not weakness, see—
It is the strength that sets me free.

My conflicting right and left brain

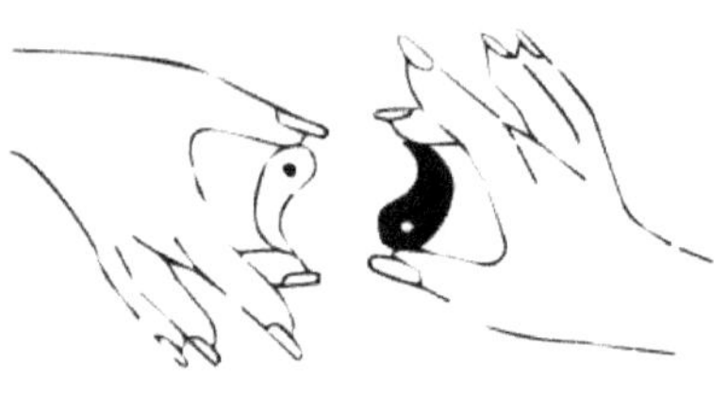

In the quiet corner of my mind's expanse,
Two dancers twirl in a strange, silent dance.
The left, a maestro, with logic defined,
Maps out the world with precision aligned.

Numbers and letters, a systematic world,
Where algorithms linger and theories are
unfurled.
It calculates dreams, it processes fears,
Timelines and logic, it neatly adheres.

Yet, oh, the right, with its colors so bright,
It paints in broad strokes, igniting the night.
An artist at heart, it wanders and plays,
In realms of imagination, it frolics and sways.

Where the left builds a bridge, the right sings
a song,
In a tapestry woven where both might belong.
The left charts the course through the stormy
terrain,
While the right finds the beauty in each drop
of rain.

Together they battle, a constant intrigue,
One finds the path, the other the league.
In this clashing theater, I sometimes feel lost,
As I juggle their whispers and ponder the
cost.

For balance is woven into the fabric of
thought,
In the dance of the dual, a treasure is sought.
So I breathe in the chaos, the push and the
pull,
In the fusion of contrasts, my spirit is full.

Right and left, a paradox grand,
A symphony played by an unseen hand.
With every embrace of reason and art,
I find the harmony nestled in my heart.

Till My Last Breath

In the whispers of the evening glow,
Where dreams and reality intertwine and
flow,
I'll dance with the shadows, a fleeting wraith,
Holding tight to each moment, till my last
breath.

With every heartbeat, a story unfolds,
In the tapestry of life, both brave and bold.
Each twist in the journey, every tear that I've
shed,
Marks a path of resilience, a song in my head.

The sun may dip low, casting long silhouettes,
But in twilight's embrace, I'll harbor no
regrets.
For love is a fire that never dims,
And in the warmth of its glow, my spirit
swims.

Through laughter and sorrow, through trials
and strife,
I cherish the colors that paint this life.
For in every heartbeat, and every sigh,
Resides a truth that shall never die.

I wander through valleys, I climb every peak,
In the arms of the wild, my soul finds its peak.
The breeze carries whispers of those I've
adored,
Their voices echo softly, like songs from a
chord.

So here's to the moments, both bitter and
sweet,
To the faces of strangers, to friends that I
meet.
With a heart full of memories, a spirit so free,
I'll cherish this journey, forever it'll be.

And when the stars gather, in the velvet of night,
I'll gaze at their brilliance, a glorious sight.
For until the last breath, my flame will persist,
A testament to living, in love, I'll insist.

Be your own competition

In a world where shadows cast their doubts,
Where whispers echo with fear and shouts,
I turn my gaze not to the race ahead,
But to the voice within, where courage is
bred.

I lace my shoes with dreams untold,
Each step is a promise, each moment bold.
No rivals lurking, no others in sight,
Just me against me, in the dawn's soft light.

The mirror reflects both scars and grace,
A portrait of trials, a journey to trace.
With every heartbeat, I chart my course,
Drawing strength from within, a powerful force.

I rise with the sun, embrace the unknown,
For competition's a choice, yet I walk alone.
The climb may be steep, the road may twist,
But I find my rhythm in the fog and the mist.

Each stumble a lesson, each fall a refrain,
In the symphony of struggle, I dance in the rain.
For every small victory, no matter how slight,
Is a testament forged in the heart of the fight.

So, here in the silence, where ambition
thrives,
I nurture the fire, the spark that survives.
Be my compass, my guiding star bright,
In this journey of one, I embrace my light.

For the only true battle, the only true quest,
Is the one against doubt, the journey to rest.
In a world full of noise, I find my song,
Be your competition; that's where you belong.

I am a work in progress

With quiet shadows, the dawn of my
becoming,
I stand, a canvas still unfolding,
Every brushstroke whispers stories,
Of trials faced and dreams unfolding.

With each mistake, a lesson learned,
With every fall, the heart has yearned,
To rise again, to stretch, to grow,
An ever-evolving, vibrant flow.

I paint with hues of doubt and hope,
Finding strength in the ways I cope,
The shadows dance, the light takes flight,
In this mosaic of day and night.

The past, a river that shaped my course,
Its currents fierce, yet I found my source,
In love, in laughter, in tears, I've cried,
Each moment a wave, a turning tide.

I gather fragments, shards of light,
To forge a path from darkness to bright,
Imperfect seams stitched with grace,
A tapestry woven in time and space.

I am a question, a quest, a plea,
A soul in search of all I can be,
An unfinished song, a whispered prayer,
Each note is a promise, a breath of air.

So here I stand, in the grand design,
Embracing the journey as truly mine,
A work in progress, forever in flight,
Crafting my story, with love as my guide.

What do you see in the Mirror?

In the mirror's gaze, a world unfolds,
A dance of light and shadows bold.
Reflection whispers secrets deep,
Of dreams long buried, and thoughts we keep.

A tapestry of time and grace,
Lines of laughter, etched on the face.
Eyes that sparkle with stories told,
A heart that beats, both fierce and bold.

A fleeting glimpse, a moment's freeze,
The joy, the sorrow, life's sweet tease.
Fragments of a thousand days,
In fleeting glances, a soul's malaise.

What do I see? The weight I bear,
The hopes that rise, the silent prayer.
Yet in that glass, a spark ignites,
A spirit soaring, chasing heights.

With every wrinkle, every scar,
The journey shaped me, no matter how far.
A myriad of shades of laughter and tears,
A portrait painted with all my fears.

So here I stand, before this glass,
Embracing the present, letting the past pass.
For in this mirror, I find my truth,
A tapestry is woven from the threads of
youth.

In moments still, the face reflects,
The beauty found in life's defects.
What do I see in the mirror's light?
A warrior in the shadows, ready for flight.

Through your eyes my child

In the quiet dawn where dreams ignite,
A child stirs softly, wrapped in the light,
With wide-eyed wonder, they gaze at the sky,
Awakening magic, where hopes begin to fly.

Each tiny heartbeat a rhythm of grace,
A world unfolding, a dance in its place,
Through laughter and tears, in joy and strife,
They teach me about living, the essence of
life.

With questions like petals, they scatter the
air,
Discovering secrets, as fragile as care,
In the garden of wisdom, they plant every
thought,
Innocence blooming, in lessons I've sought.

Through their eyes, I see colors anew,
The laughter of rainbows, the whispers of
blue,
Each moment a canvas, each day a new page,
In this beautiful story, we wander, we age.

So I lean down to listen, to learn from their
song,
With every shared giggle, with every sweet
throng,
For in our reflection, a mirror unfolds,
In the heart of my child, my own truth is told.

Slow Down, Take a Pause

Slow down, take a pause, and breathe the air,
In a world that rushes, find a moment rare.
Amid the hustle, the constant chase,
Seek a stillness, a tranquil space.
Slow down, let the heart find peace,
In the gentle quiet, let worries cease.
For in the rush, we often lose,
The simple joys, the subtle cues.
Take a pause, let the world unwind,
In the silence, true clarity you'll find.
Let the moments of stillness heal,
The weary soul, the heart that feels.
Slow down, watch the sunset's glow,
Feel the calm as the day turns slow.

In the quiet of the evening's hue,
Find a place where dreams come true.
Take a pause, within the day,
In the rush, find a gentle way.
To appreciate the life you lead,
And nourish the heart's quiet need.
Slow down, listen to the birds' sweet song,
In the calm, where you truly belong.
Let each breath be a soothing balm,
In the stillness, find your calm.
Take a pause, embrace the now,
In the present, find your vow.
To cherish each moment, let it be,
A reminder of life's simplicity.
Slow down, take a pause, and let the world fade,
In the quiet moments, let your spirit be remade.
For in the stillness, you will see,
The beauty of life's serenity.

My Blood is Olive green

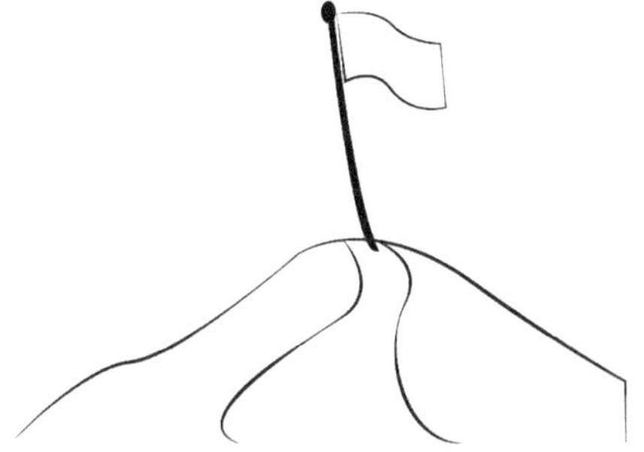

My blood is olive green, it flows with pride,
A soldier's pulse, where honor resides.
Not red with rage, nor blue with fear,
But the hue of courage, steadfast and clear.
It courses through veins like a silent vow,
To serve, to protect, to never bow.
Each drop is a symbol, a story untold,
Of sacrifice made, of hearts turned bold.
In battle's roar or the still of the night,
It fuels my resolve, and my will to fight.
Not for glory, not for fame,
But for the flag, the sacred name.
Olive green is the shade of peace,
Yet stands its ground when wars don't cease.
A bridge of hope, a shield of trust,
Carrying dreams through the winds of dust.

My blood is olive green, forever true,
For my nation, I give all, to renew.
In its flow, a promise serene—
To live, to die, with blood olive green.

Manthan

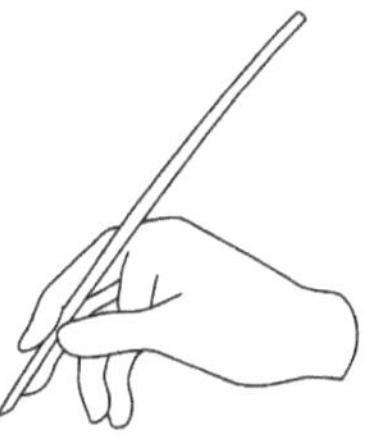

In the churn of life, the *Manthan* begins,
A dance of shadows, virtues, and sins.
Deep within the ocean of thought,
The nectar of truth and poison is caught.
Waves of doubt and tides of despair,
Collide with hope in the midnight air.
Questions rise like a storm untamed,
Seeking answers, no soul can name.
The mind a vessel, the heart a flame,
Through trials and tempests, never the same.
Each churn reveals what lies beneath,
A glimpse of strength, a buried sheath.
The poison burns, the nectar heals,
The duality of life, the balance revealed.
For every storm, there's a calm to find,
In every chaos, a peace entwined.

Manthan is more than a struggle or strife,
It's the soul's journey, the essence of life.
To churn is to grow, to rise, to fall,
And in the process, discover it all.
Let the churn continue, let the waters rage,
For within the chaos, we turn the page.
Through *Manthan*, we find what's truly divine,
The elixir of being, your soul, and mine.

Gratitude Creates Magic

In the quiet dawn where whispers play,
Gratitude blooms in the softest way.
A sunbeam's touch on a dewdrop's face,
Transforms the mundane into a sacred space.

With each breath drawn, a treasure unfolds,
In the heart's embrace, a story is told.
The warmth of a smile, the kindness of hands,
In the tapestry woven, our spirit expands.

A simple "thank you," a glance shared bright,
Turns shadows to light, ignites the night.
In moments of stillness, we find our song,
In the rhythm of gratitude, we all belong.

Like petals unfurling, like rivers that flow,
Magic ignites in the heart's gentle glow.
For every small blessing, no matter how
slight,
Is a spark in the darkness, a beacon of light.

So gather these moments, let them take flight,
For gratitude weaves wonders, both tender
and bright.
In the dance of existence, we rise and we
sway,
Creating pure magic in the simplest way.

Hear What I Don't Say

In the silence where shadows dwell,
Words unspoken weave their spell.
A whisper brushed by fleeting air,
The heart's soft cadence, stripped and bare.

Look closely at the lines I trace,
In fleeting glances, find my grace,
For in the pauses, truths align,
In the quiet, thoughts entwine.

Beneath the surface, currents flow,
In every sigh, a tale to know,
The weight of silence, heavy, profound,
In the absence of sound, my soul is found.

Listen deep, not just with ears,
But with the heart that knows my fears,
For every smile that lights my face,
Hides echoes of a secret place.

I speak in colors, vibrant and bright,
Yet shadows linger in the light,
The laughter dances, yet it hides,
A fragile world where quiet abides.

So hear what I don't say, my friend,
In the spaces where our truths blend.
For in the unsaid, the real resides,
A universe where love confides.

Hold my silence in your hands,
A tapestry of uncharted lands.
In every pause, let understanding play,
And hear the heart that longs to say.

Laughing at Life

I've learned to laugh at life's grand show,
To let the worries come and go,
For in each twist, each unexpected turn,
There's a lesson, there's a light to burn.

Life's a dance, a fleeting play,
Where joy and sorrow both hold sway,
But in the mix of night and day,
I choose to laugh, to find my way.

When troubles knock upon my door,
I greet them with a grin, not more,
For what's a storm but passing rain,
A moment's pause, not lasting pain?

I laugh at fate, I laugh at fear,
For in this heart, there's room to steer,
Through every trial, every test,
With laughter, I can face the rest.

The world may frown, may seem so grave,
But laughter is the way I save,
My soul from drowning in despair,
A buoyant heart that's light as air.

For life's too short to waste on woe,
To let the darkness steal the show,
So I laugh, I dance, I sing aloud,
A joyful spirit, unbowed, unbowed.

In every misstep, every fall,
I find the humor in it all,
For life's a journey, not a race,
And laughter's how I find my place.

So here I stand, with head held high,
Laughing at life, as it passes by,
For in each chuckle, in each smile,
I find the strength to walk the mile.

In the quiet chambers where shadows blend,
A battle rages, where thoughts ascend.
The heart, a tempest of wild, sweet cries,
The mind is a compass with rational ties.

The heart dances in dreams untold,
Whispers of love, both tender and bold.
It beckons forth with a vibrant thrill,
A siren's call, an enchanting will.

"Oh, dare to leap, to trust and to feel,
Embrace the chaos; let passion heal.
For life is fleeting, a moment's guise,
In the warmth of love, eternity lies."

But the mind, astute, with its watchful gaze,
Counters with logic, a cautious maze.
"Step back, dear heart, consider the road,
Life's not a melody, nor a lightened load.

Think of the burdens, the scars that remain,
The echoes of sorrow, the depth of pain.
What of the future? The paths left to tread?
With reason as a guide, tread lightly instead."

And so they clash, in this inner refrain,
The heart's fervent song versus reason's chain.
Each coin has two sides, a dance of the soul,
A pull and a push, a constant patrol.

Yet in this discord, a truth finds its place,
Both heart and mind wear a delicate grace.
For love needs the wisdom that reason can
bring,
While courage ignites what the heart dares to
sing.

So let them converse, let their voices entwine,
In the tapestry woven of both heart and
mind.
Conflict, when embraced, can lead to the
spark
That lights the way home from the depths of
the dark.

An Illusion Called Youth

Youth, a dream that feels so real,
A fleeting moment, hard to seal,
It dances wild, with reckless grace,
A masquerade, a timeless face.

In mirrors, youth reflects its glow,
A promise of forever's flow,
But underneath the surface clear,
Lies the truth we all must hear.

It whispers of invincible days,
Of endless nights and golden rays,
Yet time, the artist, works unseen,
Painting lines where youth has been.

We chase it down, this fleeting flame,
But youth, never stays the same,
An illusion spun with threads of gold,
A tale that's beautiful yet old.

In youth, we think the world is ours,
We're kings and queens with endless powers,
But soon we learn, as years go by,
That youth is just a wink, a sigh.

It fills our hearts with wild desires,
With passions, dreams, and burning fires,
But as the seasons change their tune,
We see youth fade, like the waning moon.

Yet even as it slips away,
Youth leaves behind a bright array,
Of memories sweet, of lessons learned,
Of bridges built, of pages turned.

So cherish youth, but know its name,
An illusion that won't stay the same,
A chapter in life's grand parade,
A fleeting moment, gently made.

For youth, though brief, is not the end,
But the beginning of what's yet to bend,
An illusion, yes, but one so sweet,
That paves the way for life to complete.

Friends We Lost in Life

In the garden where laughter bloomed,
We danced in the sunlight, our hearts
resumed,
But shadows crept in, whispers of doubt,
Promises faded, and love wore thin out.

In the tapestry of trust, we wove,
Threads of betrayal unraveled, ungloved,
Once vibrant colors turned muted and grey,
The friends we cherished slipped further
away.

Words that once sparkled turned brittle and
cold,
Secrets exchanged, a dagger of gold,
Innocence shattered, like glass on the floor,
Each shard is a reminder of friends we ignore.

We shared dreams beneath the vast, starry skies,
But masks slipped away, revealing the lies,
What once felt like home became distant and
strange,
The bonds we once knew would never be the
same.

Yet, through the sorrow, we learn and we
grow,
From the ashes of trust, new seeds we will sow,
For the lessons of loyalty, forged in the pain,
Will blossom again, like a soft summer rain.

So we mourn the lost, those paths we once
tread,
In the book of our lives, pages turned red,
But in every ending, a new tale will start,
As we learn to protect our fragile hearts.

Though friends may falter, and tempests may
rise,
We stand with resilience, with open eyes,
For betrayal may sting, but it will not define,
The strength we possess, the love we align.

Why Were You Born on Janmashtami?

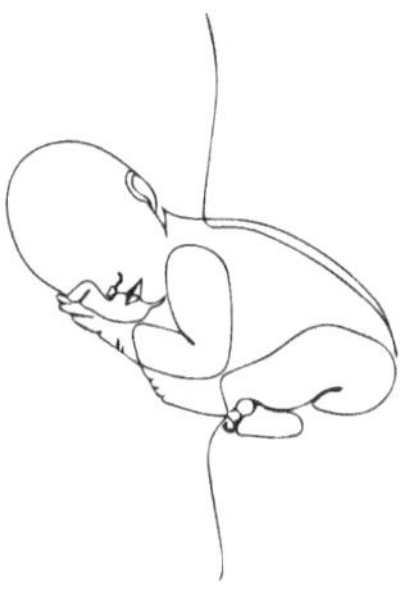

In the heart of a night, so serene and bright,
A star graced the world, a divine, wondrous
light.
Amidst the whispers of the wind and the
trees,
A child was born, bringing love with the
breeze.

On Janmashtami, echoes of joy filled the air,
As the world sang praises, casting away
despair.
With butter and sweets, the celebrations
began,
For Krishna was born, the beloved of man.

But why, dear friend, do you share this great
day?
Is it fate, is it magic, or the universe's play?
Perhaps you carry the spirit of joy,
A heart that beats freely, a soul like a buoy.

In laughter and mischief, in love and in song,
You embody the essence of where you belong.
Like Krishna, the playful, the wise and the bold,
You weave tales of wonder, more precious
than gold.

So dance in the moonlight, let your spirit take
flight,
For you were born on a night filled with light.
Embrace the connection, the magic you see,
For on Janmashtami, you were meant to be free.

In the stories of old, in the dreams yet to
come,
Remember, dear one, you're never alone.
With every step forward, in every heartbeat's
sway,
You carry the legacy of love's endless play.

9 789367 391242